LIVES

LIVES

CJ EVANS

SARABANDE BOOKS *Louisville, KY*

Publisher's Cataloging-In-Publication Data
(Prepared by The Donohue Group, Inc.)

Names: Evans, CJ, author.
Title: Lives / CJ Evans.
Description: Louisville, KY : Sarabande Books, 2022
Identifiers: ISBN 9781946448965 (paperback) | ISBN 9781946448972 (e-book)
Subjects: LCSH: Life—Poetry. | Belonging (Social psychology)—Poetry.
Universe—Poetry. | Environmental degradation—Poetry. | LCGFT: Poetry.
Classification: LCC PS3605.V3646 L58 2022 (print) | LCC PS3605.V3646 (e-book)
DDC 811/.6—dc23

Cover design by Gabriele Wilson.
Interior design by Alban Fischer.
Printed in Canada.
This book is printed on acid-free paper.
Sarabande Books is a nonprofit literary organization.

This project is supported in part by an award from the National Endowment for the Arts.
The Kentucky Arts Council, the state arts agency, supports Sarabande Books with
state tax dollars and federal funding from the National Endowment for the Arts.

For Naomi, Dahlia, and Auden

CONTENTS

INTRODUCTION

CJ Evans's beautiful book, *Lives*, explores and circles around, into, and out of what it means to be free and alive in a world where humans insist on war and environmental destruction. Evans's speaker is constantly trying to remain present in the world through deep perception and seeing, unable to free himself from his past (having served time in literal prison and the metaphorical prison of addiction). In the process, he gifts the reader with his keen perception and awakens the reader. Evans writes in "Now That the Time for Lives Getting Better Is Done": "And what else could my heart be for if not to try?" The collection renders through language a gorgeous natural and domestic landscape within a landscape that is dying—one war, one shooting, one plastic bottle at a time. *Lives* maps the apocalypse while simultaneously trying to resist it through language and life.

Lives is divided into four sections, but in some ways, it feels like one long poem. The third section, which is the most deeply steeped in human ruin, degradation, and environmental collapse, is fittingly the longest section. "I think this // is our last century," the speaker says in "At the Old Tideline." Also here is the role of the speaker as a father. Ghostly children are stitched throughout the collection, as if to say the future of the earth and its children is uncertain. Evans articulates parental concerns, both the usual and the global—saving and building an earth for them—while acknowledging his complicity, as in the poem "As yesterday and tomorrow we await war, so the news is war as always.":

> I asked what they'll do once I'm done, why alone they
> must go in this world full of thorns and scorpion holes.
>
> This world bones and salts. In the sun I lose the borders
> of my body, my smell pulls into sandstone, disappears

into washes where poisons run, beetles with bright legs,
sharp grasses and nightshades. Even still here, still trying,

still breaking, I can't change anything—this one body
is just another root struggling to slow the whole earth.

Mortality permeates all these poems. The speaker persists, what will happen when he disappears from this earth? In another poem, "In my fear for you, I fear," the speaker again laments the human proclivity toward destruction: "It's no longer just the elections, the shootings, not just / kids running from the arena. It's us: we are this maul, swinging again // again, till we split the trunk."

In the middle of *Lives* is a masterful longer poem called "Trying to Hear a Hymn to Life." Again, the word *trying*; implicit in that word is *not succeeding*. Reading this collection, I thought of Rilke, his tone of searching and existentialism. The poem begins with an extinct sabertooth tiger while the speaker ruminates on Oakland's Lake Merritt and how: "Much later, / of course they poured the concrete, cutting a teethline / across the wetland, closing Lake Merritt completely."

The genius of this poem is how it mimics a sestina or a villanelle in its recurring imagery and repetitions. Bullfrogs, the sabertooth, Oakland, a sexual predator, wildfires, caterpillars, a child, a wife, church, a neighbor. In these appearances and disappearances, the poem mimics how memory circles while changing. They are thumbnail narratives of beauty, devastation, and gravity. One experience with sexual abuse is gone just as it arises:

maybe I can be there with my wife
when my body is young again. Suddenly, through
the speaker comes "America" by Simon
and Garfunkel, and I'm at a pond in Western
Massachusetts: bullfrogs, slick grasses, another

boy pressing me to the molding bank and taking
my penis in his mouth. He has no name or face,
less real than the bullfrogs, than the liquor squeezed

from the grasses by our bodies that marks my skin,
less real than my grandfather who worked in a clock

factory, drank scotch, and smoked until he died young,
years before I was born

The nameless, faceless boy is sandwiched between the memory of a sexual encounter
and the memory of the speaker's grandfather who worked in a clock factory. The
boy reappears later in the poem: "Like bullfrogs' organs, / that young boy's mouth,
that grass, the underground fungus // ferrying for the roots, my wife, or my sleeping /
children." The assault is depicted via a synecdoche. "Trying to Hear a Hymn to Life"
is a master study in how to write a long poem and anchors the entire collection.

Throughout *Lives*, Evans exhibits great facility with imagery. In "Crow," he writes:

When I was younger and someone else
entirely I heard one calling to me

from the ledge of her building. Then
another on the radio, then another

from a knife. I heard their voices
in a cell where I was alone for a very

long time and now I hear them
in electrical sockets and in airplanes

and in the arteries in my arms.

In "Fathering in the Discord," Evans writes:

Over politics,
over toxic plastics, over sirens
and my memories of handcuffs.

I'm powerless, and know it best
when, late, I try to hear if your heart
has gone silent. I can't detect

that tangled knot, so I'm carried
like lichen is carried by a boulder,
crashing down the hillside

Other memorable lines include: "I went looking for myself who was lost," "A ghost, a free man, wearing the face I wore before I wore this one," "The bald eagles inside me are scavengers," "I have never gone / to Michigan but I believe in it," "I'm trying again what you [to the poet Lucie Brock-Broido] taught me: To build a body to tend / with witches in wet dirt," "Was this the last time / I'd lift her [the speaker's daughter]?" "Your back, long // as an untested trestle bridge. / Your neck, long as a war year," "I don't know how to tell you about / the rain. It falls as if all these woods // weren't owned," and many more.

Ultimately, this book is about trying to reconcile our many selves and the countless selves of others. We're attempting to forgive our past selves, to unknow the past, to move on, to save the world for children, to have hope, trying to make sense of the short lives we have on this earth. The book is intimate, expansive, and in moments, willfully hopeful. In the poem, "We think we're god enough to destroy it" Evans writes: "There is a price I've exacted / to live—a shadow in which nothing else could grow— / but since I'm here I'd love."

—Victoria Chang, 2021

ONE

JUPITER IS BLIND

She says something private, only
for me to hear, and as soon

as the words leave her mouth
they begin to die as ochre leaves

die, suspended for a brief time
by the atmosphere's invisible

efforts, but proceeding toward
their place amid the bones

of yesterday's forgotten animals.
The earth flexes and warps,

the borders of its logic recede.
It's not her words that speak,

but her voice, and this is her time,
but like any time, it's merely

a time, and it too will close,
as it must. If, uncounted years

from now, the light reflected off
her face has traveled to some

far place and is collected
by the alien telescope, the viewer

will see a perfect record of her,
but it won't be her. If only

she knew that it's now that
her life is important. It's her

reflected in the shine
of the animals' eyes. The whales

live in the cold ocean for her.
They speak tonight to no

other thing in history but her.
The grasses on the cliffs cling

against the wind, the seabirds
travel the coasts, and the sun

burns its own body for her.
As impossible as it seems

within all the ungovernable
enormity, she lives. At the center

of the black cavity, she's
the impulse that sparks the heart.

CROW

When I was younger and someone else
entirely I heard one calling to me

from the ledge of her building. Then
another on the radio, then another

from a knife. I heard their voices
in a cell where I was alone for a very

long time and now I hear them
in electrical sockets and in airplanes

and in the arteries in my arms. I hear
their voices come from the fireplace,

from the oven, their voices from
the crawlspace and from the cobweb

noplace within the walls. Their voices
come from tree burls and from sewers

and from all the newly empty lots,
and they ask: What if bald birds circle?

What if savages come haunting?
What if motorcycles and what if

madness? Their voices come from
leafpiles and from keyholes;

their voices come from my hands
and they ask: What if that cell is waiting?

WHAT THE SEAS WOULD MAKE US

I don't know how to tell you about
the rain. It falls as if all these woods

weren't owned. It bends the arcs
of meteorites and flies, invites

uninhibited fucking on blankets of fir
needles. That night in Harlem we didn't

kiss: this lifetime of lovely almost-but-
never pain is the rain's. I want it to riot

at my small end, loose in the flowers
that'll roof my grave. If we stop

with all these buildings and laptops
and flashing LEDs—all our

ceaseless wanting—this rain will
grow us a world new, naked and wild.

FATHERING IN THE DISCORD

Our home is porous, endlessly
inflicted. The world snaps
at its cracks, and I'm powerless

over the oceans of war that break
and break again. Powerless over
viruses and slipping cracks

in the mantle. Over politics,
over toxic plastics, over sirens
and my memories of handcuffs.

I'm powerless, and know it best
when, late, I try to hear if your heart
has gone silent. I can't detect

that tangled knot, so I'm carried
like lichen is carried by a boulder,
crashing down the hillside. My only

weaponry lives among the birches
of your ribs, my only defense
is the leap of that spotted deer.

MY RAZORWIRE

Ash the blood-
shot news.
Ash the alleys, ash
the nightsticks,

ash in flashbangs,
in Seidel, in
nonlethal.
Ash over the asphalt.

Ash the boys' bodies.
A
shhh in our blood,
shooting through.

Wish other
ways but no
other ways grown,
just shhh.

Ash the high tree
but the dirt goes on
knowing. Ashes don't
wash the history.

From far I see us
through. Ash

the northern
noose, ash the ancestry,

ash the photos.
Our allegiance
to shhh.
Not all poems are about death.

This one's
about this life:
shit, caskets, trash,
and sheltered clout.

The shout we dwindle
and the next and next.
Through our clean
hands,

our shhh, our
little kids witness
the ash we scatter.
Witness

the pages and pages
latched up and left
under ash.
The bloodshot and blood-

shed we set in
our babies
no matter the baptism.
Ash teargas,

ash taser, ash
the boys' bodies.
Ash and shhh,
but the kids

see that every tree
baptized in this ash
knows the weight
of a body.

ALONE ON THE ARK WITH SIRIUS

Out of concrete with rebar bones,
tempered glass, I-beams, and structural
bolts, the buildings are impossible.

But they grow from this same
ground, and they sway the same,
and beneath our feet, the whims

of limestone seams can undo them
also. And we will all, eventually,
be carried away by wind.

Though I know we live above ghosts
of old cities, whose inhabitants
believed what we believe,

I'm thankful for these things we make.
But the indelible mark isn't built.
It's in the wooden box of private

letters written in private years.
And not even the box and not
even the letters, but just this:

Dear CJ. Far from me, somewhere,
that thought rose in a mind
so utterly not mine. Behind the storm

frames of a remote lighthouse
she lit the wick, and its light
breaks me from the endless order.

SINCE THE LAST SHOOTING,
UNTIL THE NEXT SHOOTING

How could we not keep cowering
in the locked closet, our furious

blood a sound we're wishing silent
as the monster comes to report

on the end he sees here. How
could we not crawl to cradle

every spent body in the hall, learn
the weight of trying to take

them up, and how we can't.
How could we not return, day

after day, to line the school fence
with our bodies, to refill the closet

with our bodies, to spill the tables
and shiver beneath them, day

after day, to break holes in the walls
where the holes were, to find, day

after day, some way to interrupt
the processes of the sun, day

after day all of it break all
of it until all that's left is the locked

closet where between reports
we hear our blood.

A LESSON ABOUT SUICIDE

I sit our small children down
to tell them about gravity.

That their bodies have gravity.
That they pull, however finely,

on every other body in the universe.
I want them to know the inherent

element of their material,
that their atoms could gather

together with the atoms of you
and me to be part of a star

someday. But I end up describing
the deep parts of the ocean,

where worms gather around
volcanic vents to eat poison

that floods from breakages
in the mantle, where fire billows

from the skeleton of the place
where they, just like you and I,

have to make a home.
I sit our small children down

to tell them about habitable
exoplanets. That I'm certain

there's more than just this,
and though I doubt we will hear

from them, I feel less adrift
knowing they, too, must

wonder at the dark dome,
and it's the same dark dome.

Life cascades ever larger;
there's nothing to do but love

and continue. But I keep talking
about the abyssal plain,

whale falls and marine snow,
unbearable pressure. About

the lightless trenches where
it's forbidden to all but a few,

and I wish I could tell them
what it is you see there.

TWO

TRYING TO HEAR A HYMN TO LIFE

—*after Donnelly & Schuyler*

One story goes that the sabertooth stood right there,
then the shellmound where terns and cranes high-stepped, plucking
overlooked morsels from the bivalve waste. Much later,
of course they poured the concrete, cutting a teethline
across the wetland, closing Lake Merritt completely.

Aquafina bottles now bonk gently against
the downy underbellies of Canada geese.
Near the fountain's west intake, there's an eddy haloed
by crinkled seagrass where all types of refuse
collect: plastic cutlery, outlawed bags, condoms.

I can't see the lake from here, but I believe
it still is. Just as I believe in the shellmounds
I'll never see, the sabertooth, that the flat moon
is actually a sphere. I believe as I do
in this tabletop you can't touch: wood pulp crushed

in a hydraulic press with glue. It looks like slabbed
oak from an old tree, but that's one lie. That lie still
not making the whole fact of the table a lie.
I believed it when I heard my house was once part
of a redwood grove that covered the hill up there.

That it talked, shared, attacked, or consoled via fungal
mycelium. The roots signaled, sent nitrogen

and magnesium to their failing family
members through that ever-entwining vinework.
What mayday did the trees send when poor men came and cut

them down, piled the naked, shamed trunks, red and knotted,
onto sleds and slid them here, where they were hewn
and riftsawn into boards? I've seen the sawtooth marks
on oddly sized planks within the walls, but now
the drywall is back up, any proof is hidden.

I'm alerted. I look, recoil, blacken the screen.
The house is sinking into the streambed that haunts
the stability of the soil. The cemented
stream once fed the marsh for the now-absent terns.
But if it rains hard enough the stream returns, running

the street curb to curb, biblical, reclaiming
this city for the god. But in the morning
it's as if there had only ever been this dry,
disorderly, destroyed place. Outside the window
now a thin caterpillar, what kind I don't know,

eats the leaf of my hedgeplant. The caterpillars
of my youth were wild-haired, black and yellow, slow
accordion approximates of bumblebees.
My mother says when I was four I ate one.
Some days I'm able to look at something other

than what most demands. To look away from what pings
to the caterpillars, the studs, the semi-wild
turkeys that escaped their rose garden home a few
blocks down toward the lake. The female stands in traffic,
the male puffs and plumes at the median, making

his ridiculous call. I won't laugh, though, because
I'm in love too, I hoot my own ugly calls . . .
I believe it was me who once stood on a beach
of agates. I believe in this as much as god
or biology, which is to say, a bit less

than to make a bet with it against a bullet,
but enough. I call it belief, but it's purposefully,
wondrously unexamined. Today as I try
to see this caterpillar, there are wildfires
in Marin, the air outside a choke, ash of lives

is senselessly lofted as if love letters lost
in bottles beneath the sea, brought here illegible
and alone. But the wildflowers and grasses will
germ again. Grass and wildflowers the things that'll come
back even after we've done what we'll do to end

us and gone, the grass and wildflowers will come back
to be a hide for what rodents remain, and rain
will wet it green, and new roots will weave again
into a new language, and new mushrooms will carry
the history of what we did in measurable

isotope levels that will be forever
ignored by the wildflowers and grasses. I believe
this too, and I have no proof. I have never gone
to Michigan but I believe in it. My daughter
has told me there's only one living sabertooth

and it lives in her imagination. That's some
kind of real, the same kind to me as Botswana,
the same as this tabletop or the parked Nissan

overlooking Lake Washington. Not that different
than, beyond the hedge and caterpillar, mica

enlivening the stucco of my neighbor's tan
and ill-kept home if I choose the angle to see.
On the TV through her window they're showing
a picture, pulled from Facebook, the one with the flag.
I quickly open a book close at hand, reading:

"Of the wide world I stand alone, and think." I stop,
for that's enough for now . . . Today, no longer
belonging to me, but still *here* in me is that
attic where our bodies first met, the smell of dirt
we made is still in that air, kept always, and if

I choose it maybe I can be there with my wife
when my body is young again. Suddenly, through
the speaker comes "America" by Simon
and Garfunkel, and I'm at a pond in Western
Massachusetts: bullfrogs, slick grasses, another

boy pressing me to the molding bank and taking
my penis in his mouth. He has no name or face,
less real than the bullfrogs, than the liquor squeezed
from the grasses by our bodies that marks my skin,
less real than my grandfather who worked in a clock

factory, drank scotch, and smoked until he died young,
years before I was born. The antics of even
the brightest stars are so distant—equally as real
to me as the sabertooth within her . . . Ants climb
the chimneyside to the right of the window

advancing on some crack in my home. Sometimes
I can look at something muted. Not the gold-edged
paper or the amateurish illustrations
of the bible my father brought home from Vietnam,
but the glue and fine stitching. The smell of who he

once was. The ants, individually, twitch.
I paid a man to put out poison that didn't work.
Sometimes I can turn from the display and dwell in
something frivolous like my love for the consonants
of construction: cripple walls, tenpennys, flashing

and sheathing. One ant has gotten in, antennae
plotting the sill. I pinch it gently and tip it
into my mouth. What feels like panic on my tongue.
I spit dryly, see nothing come out, and the ant
is gone. The body of the last sabertooth,

my daughter's, will also melt in tar alongside
its prey as she ages, be boiled for Subarus,
iPhones. For me—sitting under this light alone.
It seemed seconds ago the house was cacophonous
as my kids ate chicken thighs with their hands—

cartilage spinning webs between their fingers
as they ripped the salted and fatty skin with sharp
new teeth, and I had thought: What if I just let them
stay feral and knot-haired? When they found that albino
salamander under a rock in the yard—if

I had let them take it in their potentially
violent hands and open a more dangerous,

perhaps vivid life. What I once did to bullfrogs.
Over the counter fruit flies that live for eleven
hours, mouthless, stomachless, their life a matter

of condensed energy as if quasars circling
the black hole massively centered on the aging
bananas on the fabricated quartz countertop.
There's a code there I won't decipher, something
I'll never learn. They lay eggs I can't see

under the skin of fruit we eat. "America"
falls silent. I can only be here, trying
to see, at least for now, whatever doesn't alert,
but on the radio such same virulent
words are being spoken again by the same man . . .

Damn I wish I knew the names of flowers. Jorie
knows all the flowers, and in knowing them can mourn
them in ways I'm unable. There are fat blossoms
on the hedge, pink and white with little yellow
filaments within, hiding behind the blush

as a gold tooth behind the cheek. When the blossoms
fall they rot fast, and I see them most often when . . .
on the radio now an astronaut is saying
you can lose your arm in a shadow in space,
the shadows, without particles to diffuse light

into them, are absolute. As I age I find
myself more and more humbled in the *prospect*
of a god. Just all this stuff I won't get to know
and how I'm less comfortable in sureness.
There is more land in Oakland than there used to be,

sand was scooped from high places and deposited
to reshape the shore, which fights back slowly, sure
of its ultimate dominance. And I see where
the ocean once held, what it will hold again
one day. I am relieved somehow by seeing it.

My daughter named her sabertooth Toothy because
she's seven. I believe her when she tells me it
follows her, docile but vengeful. Everywhere new
buildings are rising—their construction invisible
if I look too directly, as if they're ashamed

to grow. Their skeletons stand on sand backfill,
and faults ripple the earth, and they *will* someday fall,
as unlikely as it seems, but that only
increases my awe of them. Like bullfrogs' organs,
that young boy's mouth, that grass, the underground fungus

ferrying for the roots, my wife, or my sleeping
children. A block toward Lake Merritt is the shelter
where I catch the bus that carries me across rock
hung from roped steel and as I ride, the light off
those new skyscrapers is a type of demand, but

I choose the gentler light from the bayside instead.
Will there be, I hope, some time before the end
when I'll sit without this unnameable burn to see?
I don't know where I was when my father and I
watched a field of three thousand sandhill cranes take flight,

but I could take you to the place on Lake Washington
where I saw my first dead body. A few Canada
geese would rise, honking. My neighbor moves in her

window past the hedge, pulling a beer from the fridge
through the lattice of dark leaves, walking gracefully

in front of the TV—on which a family
hugs and is broken, incomplete from now on—
then she walks out of my sense, leaving me to watch
grief. I was seventeen and stood above the floating
thing in the moonlight, stoned and unsure. The lake

was always deeper after that, full of fingers.
I don't know what to believe about that body,
gone now from me, like so many others. The soft
body as we lay entwined in the attic,
the smell we made, the cigarettes not masking it

but mixing. The cranes thick in the field as if they
were the field, its dirt, its roots, its char from the burn
to resettle the carbon. How they lurched and rose
as paper ash, gray and rare and then gone.
I look at myself in the bevel-framed mirror

on the bookshelf, my eyes are a dirtier
color than I know them, and I'm brought back to how
I always loved agates best, their trapped milk, the veins
of shyest blues or reds that mar their uniformity
and make them substandard gems but better rocks.

I picked the ones that struck me best along the shores
of the Puget Sound when I was young, without any
reasoning beyond a vague pulling—probably
hastening erosion of the shoreline, but I'm
only human, too. The sabertooth, my daughter

knows that it isn't in the real world; it exists
completely for her without her needing it
to be here for the rest of us. At the agate
beaches, if I happened to look up past the band
of seaweed that hiccupped with lice, the ocean

was always too big, full of nothingness,
brine and pressure, even less knowable than
the lake. As implacable as the interior
life of another person, even my wife—she's
really somewhere too deep to submerse to. Her legs

are wrapped in the sheets as she sleeps: the hard bones
of Naomi's hips and quasars and neck, and ice
on comets, comets made of ice, falling, how
I've never even seen a fox in the wild, I've seen
many possums, but only ever one alive . . .

The bald eagles inside me are scavengers
with dirty feathers. My neighbor passes again—
I mark here her slow rhythm of consumption.
Behind her on the TV the telescopic
lens jiggles, catches on them running through the parking

lot, hair and clothes whipped by the helicopter's blades
as it settles in a vulturish arc as if
smelling them. I sat in a pew every morning
for years, but I don't know any of the hymns anymore,
but when I pass the church down the street toward the lake,

plácid in its concrete enclosing, I hear
the music and I almost have to sit *joyful*

joyful. All the hymns, I think, say at least: life.
I love the guileless hope the old songs have, belief
at the base that it isn't all some lie. It could

be. An alien computer, trick of dying
synapses. Maybe I'm not even my electric
mechanisms, dynamos and whirligigs
whinging in the solid-seeming mass of my head.
But whatever this is that's mine I'll take and eat

all of, and choose, today, to see to what doesn't
often demand enough, to what might not need
to be real to be mine: sexually dimorphic
mealybugs on the rubbertree plant in the corner,
the long grain of white oak floorboards. I built planters

from redwood to raise the vegetable beds above
the dirt that's poisoned by lead, and it's late winter,
soon we'll shake some small seeds into our children's hands—
these children who have never been not their own, some
part strangers as soon as they speak—and tell them

from these dots sunflowers and tomatoes and squash
will grow. The green beans came in well last year, the peppers
had some rot. If nothing grows, we'll say the mystery
remains beyond us, and leave it: we too are on
a ball of ice falling, we too are falling

away at an ever-increasing pace, cooling
rapidly, losing the hyperactivity
in our atoms. Al Green comes on and I'm reminded
of something, but it slips past without resting.
Bald-faced hornets in my yard defend their paper

nests, but I don't know what they look like. In the tree
I see black-bored holes where life made a home,
where it hatched in the dark and I stick my finger
in, hoping to feel. Sometimes what demands *demands*
and the names we've given to abstract them—Parkland,

Santa Fe, Springfield, Columbine—strip themselves
open and I crawl back into Newton on bloody
knees. Scared kids hiding in the dark and then my hands
are anvils for a while. But sometimes I can turn
from how it is demanded I see, and I can

set aside the incessant and empty, and sing
their names from on my bloody knees. I can ignore
whatever's been decided about poetry,
about nations or weapons or grace. Let nature
be the only empire. Let the barriers we

raised slip beneath the breakwater, and let this home
be the murmuring forest again. I know
cold water is sweet in the middle of the night,
Naomi's necklaces and perfume bottles make
music on the dresser when the earth quakes. I know

many parts are dark. And tomorrow there could be
some other world. I'm relieved that there are fewer
humans to come than have been—we plummet the slope
of our dominion's curve. How, at the oceanfront,
hands heavy with agates, I always watch for proof

of the wind, all the things it bends. The cars on the bridge
sway beneath the drivers' hands, the kites, the grasses,
the waves all strain differently. Through my neighbor's

window wrong things come from wrong mouths, demanding
again, but wind is what strikes me from listening

again, and tomorrow, maybe, I can rise
in a place as unlikely as this one but less
ravening, and the hymn will ring and the harm
we let be, we are, we demand, will starve. The lake
is past my neighbor's house—the lake is hidden but

the lake is there. As am I: Someone here who once
stood watching the sun rise and refract in prison
fences keeping me in; woke in a black row
between high German corn stalks, insects exploring
my nose and eyes. Woke on the Pacific, the boat's

porthole split between the early sun warming
the atmosphere and the placid cold of the ocean
underneath, which will not be broken. I woke
beside my wife in Croatia, in Portland, in
an Oakland where the shellmounds of the Ohlone

have not been cemented, where the wetland remains
and if it's all I have, even if it's all just
something I've invented, I take it nonetheless
as mine. I once woke to the huffing of lions
outside the camp, and I woke to my breathless son,

his lips blue, but the next morning I still got to
have him. I once woke to another lake, far
in the mountains, with nobody there to prove me.
I choose to believe that Naomi is upstairs
even though she's silent, as my children are,

asleep, silent, but still with me. I'll distrust
even the fire of the sun and choose to see outside
the pain that eats through the borders of its moment,
wolfing everything to the children. I'll choose
some other: the sandhill crane's neck, the red aphids

industrious in the garden, the sabertooth
that is real in some better world within her.
I only wish those kids hadn't had to be scared.
That we had found some way to, if nothing more human,
not let them be scared. Today I try to turn

into certainty that someone now holds them tight.
My daughter walks through the kitchen just upstairs,
murmuring for Toothy. It's not a show—it's not
for me, and I can look at the caterpillar,
at the bees riffling the yellow stamens, at wind

or wasps or racoons in their deep dens, and not
what forces its way in. Maybe I could hold them
myself, for just a second. It's dark. The type of night
for storms. I crawl back into Sandy Hook on my
bloody knees, knowing that I never stopped crawling

since, but before I reach those bodies that I'd see—
if I saw nothing else—I would see held, I hear
a bird. No, not a bird but a keen like a bird,
but scorching, a siren, which demands I turn
away and I am someplace else again in noise.

THREE

AN ORCHARD IS A FOREST WE BROKE

Walk with me the rows and whir: poor trees poor trees
poor wildness clipped, fruit plucked, ugly branches robbed
of the weight of little animals. Pears rot around the roots,
blind black eyes in yellow skin infolding, eaten from inside

by neglect and wet. Along down the row and earth bends
away from them toward naked dirt between, and here,
in the cold cradle of winter, we wear high vulcanized boots,
and I work hard each day to remain in the world with you.

WE THINK WE'RE GOD ENOUGH
TO DESTROY IT

so it warms to be rid of us.

Little leverets grown
long-limbed, we've spread too far, so a fox is sent.

But the fox is us, too, culling us even as we starve
from the abundance of us.

*

There is a price I've exacted
to live—a shadow in which nothing else could grow—
but since I'm here I'd love.

Not in some time
come or gone, but only now

while what owns us
lets us, before it burns us off like ticks.

IF IT GIVES, IT GIVES

I might cut a path through this high grass, shoots
downright red with life, damp with it. Leaves trampling

over each other like bodies on the beachheads of history,
their color a currant against the breakdown of those

beneath. Ash drifts as moths. Let me follow this path
through this same field again sometime. Will I still find

all this so hard? Will I stop to lick the copper where grass
slashes living lines in my legs? Will I feel it then?

STOPPING IN DEATH VALLEY

I've pulled to the apron of the tarmac line disappearing
    into a desert, doors wide to the night of coyotes
    who hum and break branches

that aren't there, always behind. A man on the radio
    speaks slowly about mingled particles. If one
    is excited from its state

in this place then that one—cousin, lover,
    double—rises in its own place to complete
    what they learned all of ago

at the outset, before anything came together
    into these larger things. We've let our growing
    distract us from the fact

that we grow more impossibly remote. Are you
    sleeping well tonight? Are you also looking
    for some life amid bracken

and terrible sounds that recede back to their terrible
    distance? Maybe there's a lab beneath this dead
    place where they'd strap us

down, feed us masses of photons through lenses,
    mingle our clouds in a laser, shoot us
    into the groaning emptiness

so someday, after all the days have been counted
    and the rotations are at rest, I'll feel you again
    and you'll feel the impact too.

TO A WILD PLACE

Shattered silverfish bodies in the vanity globes,
they know me. How I hate my body, how it's been

abandoning me. How I look up to the light to not
see mirrored back the emptying cup of my jaw,

the blight, the thin red running the sclera
as a river, blooded delta, ridden with crow.

I study their remnants instead, shaken to nightdust,
then close the light and into dark our bodies I sew.

A FEW QUESTIONS FOR YOU

Why we even bother to be in our bodies if

we just aim to break them. Why glyphosate,

why kill bees. Whales and all those girls

along the roads. Why drones, blacksites,

bumpstocks. Why the boy, discarded in the sand,

so close to our unnatural supermarkets. Tell me:

how do I keep cutting these flowers

when they cover so many crowded graves.

NIGHT TERRORS IN AMERICA

If I were to try, I'd begin with awe, with iron core, mantle, the oceans
full of secretive things. Land just a glimpse of skin, deliciously unblemished.
Then closer: ferns and fjords and sliding glaciers. But I'd end up leaning in
to trace walls, borders, touch a finger to the men practicing their sicknesses
and landmines. Scratching topsoil to lever out the hydrogen bombs and gas
chambers they'd have history's dirty mirror forget. I still don't want
to leave my want for this place behind. If I were to try again: whales,
white spiders in caves, and all those simple stones that carry no trace of us.

AFTER THE IPHONE

To fight back the ocean we use trees.
Plant them wherever money's made

from money. In our expanding forests,
lustful, our bodies molt, flense, go wet

in the oxygen-rich air. In new soil we
germinate again, come together again.

Leaves stick to our new skins, dress us
as earthworms, as oaks, as chanterelles.

METAMORPHOSIS

I went looking for myself who was lost. He'd ceased his crying and cutting
and kissing, all his ways of signaling. In our unmoving factories I looked,

amid Oakland's rotted piers, into the light of the internet we taught to lie.
He glanced up and all his gods were dead, replaced with today's smaller gods.

I heard he died, drunk, tossed himself in the river. I hope he's in a place
where the horizon pins the stormclouds. I hope he won't ever stop loving you.

Maybe he lies under a cedar's canopy, away from guns, away from causes
and blood. A ghost, a free man, wearing the face I wore before I wore this one.

DOWN WHERE LIVES ARE LIVED

Here within the swarm of war, this now-unending war,
underfoot with the fetters and fallen, grows some sweetpea

and one heavy calla lily. Their roots mingle with worms—
brave biology in the math bracken of war, where each person's

shot artery, punctured liver, is just a number. Except here
she is, still breathing, each slower than the one before,

each trying a name, each pushing petals and a few leaves.
A stem is bent by her life before the stem unbends.

COYOTE IN THE DESERT,
GASOLINE SPLASHED AROUND

A lost rent check; a felon; I am pliers. But gathered up by your sharp
beak I've been rewoven. How you ply me with spit and physics. Finding myself
laid over your knees, too far gone to mend but open, denuded, resurrected.

Unidentifiable to myself without my gin and fists. Taken up by you, I'm still
a dead branch but now a brace. I admit I'm scared. I admit I am needle, I admit
I am ozone, arsenic, flint, and opiate. I admit it's nothing but sinew

you take with you, catgut, mossrot, but you bite in, clean me to the bones,
and build a break to weather this world where I've only been a weapon.

THERE WERE NEVER ANY ANSWERS
AND THAT'S THE ONLY ONE.

Let there be no bodies if only in these bent lines,
my beloved. I would dress this place in mosses,

would please, would armor us in dirt and bark. If I
crawl and writhe in talc and salt. If I say it. Please.

But you'll never be with me again, because bodies
stay torn. What they held stays gone. If I plead: Let

at least, let at least nests. Bright eggs to replace
lungs in the ribcage of your body that stays torn.

TODAY YOU WILL NOT DIE
A HORRIBLE DEATH

No drowning no opiates. No body no hands in this body no fingers in this body
brutish no. No bombers, no. Neither enemies nor entreaty against force: instead
say *eased* to an ending. Say *eased into it*. No sharp report no red lights lit
    , underground no claxon no. Say *a type*

of mending, even if it was too late for mending. Not like an animal left to street, god
not like the little ones with cracked lips. No drowning, no teeth, no stutter in aim,
no simple neglect no. No hands in this body, no bouncing betties sculpting
    this field, no new virus. Say: *the light there*

and a smell like strawberries. Say *simply* even *snow*. No ordnance no, no knife
no, please no knife in my body no kalashnikov suicide strychnine no. Please
    no. No more hands in my body.

UNLOCK

They say beyond locks guns call and faults crack curbs,

skitter buses; but Naomi, my mind runs at your neck

bent over a book rather than out, where trains

rustle with hands jostling secrets in pockets. Let's unbolt

our locks to let in dangerous boys and their loud noise

if they'd come. Let locks untumble and lie down, you

and I, wildly unwalled and naked in air that comes in

full of salt and some humid premonition of sun.

AS YESTERDAY AND TOMORROW WE AWAIT WAR, SO THE NEWS IS WAR AS ALWAYS.

I asked what they'll do once I'm done, why alone they
must go in this world full of thorns and scorpion holes.

This world bones and salts. In the sun I lose the borders
of my body, my smell pulls into sandstone, disappears

into washes where poisons run, beetles with bright legs,
sharp grasses and nightshades. Even still here, still trying,

still breaking, I can't change anything—this one body
is just another root struggling to slow the whole earth.

IN MY FEAR FOR YOU, I FEAR

even you, little doe. I can't anymore. Among invasive eucalyptus,
walking on the husks of dead bees, I'd go back whenever,
whenever: even to the curbs and cuts and bottles of my youth.

Little doe, we're such slick animals and we're everywhere, every
where now: It's no longer just the elections, the shootings, not just
kids running from the arena. It's us: we are this maul, swinging again

again, till we split the trunk. Us: deer that bite the shoots, pull the roots,
taking. We take into our teeth, all the way to new buds and through.

CLIFFS DOWN TO THE SEA

Any monarch, dead and pinned, maintains its beauty, fragile as some

mineral, only lacking its flutter, its flight away.

And one monarch, dressing

a naked limb among the million mottled bodies that maraud the coast, would

die unmourned—it's only when they've almost all died we see. 87

percent fewer monarchs migrated this year.

Most simply rest in milkweed,

eschewing the eucalyptus; caterpillars stay unborn unpupated unliquified

and unwinged. The last few don't know they're alone—

then we enclose

them for us. We kill them all except these, then these we force to live.

ADDICT EXERCISE

Sometimes alone, merging with some forest
or another, I try knowing what it would be

to be broken, so I pretend you died. I contrive
a tragedy—mirror-shards, pillbottles, pine

boards. I convince myself there's no other way
to know, except to stop going on, how devotedly

I would not go on. And that's how I'm lost,
even when it's you that comes to recover me.

IN THIS POEM WITHOUT YOU
I'M ALONE AS URANIUM ORE

still unripened in the ground. Alone as a nickel, wet
roadkill in the stormdrain, the last shorebird pecking
at nothing in the sand. Come home a last time.
This shamed, this used, this american body of mine
is near-done. Or I'm done with all it has become,
being american. I know I know, but come one more
time. I'm as alone as a dry bathtub, as unatmosphered
earth. I pace in here, as alone as a rabid animal is alone.

AT THE OLD TIDELINE

Better than I know people, I know now why piers shed splinters,
bow at buckling knees, why they settle into a wanted rest.

I know the ocean's white teeth, its memory of bodies. The line
where land ends, and how that line advances. I think this

is our last century. Too late we counted up the cost
of our smokestacks' carbon haloes. I never thought, as we lay

among the low breakers, twisting in foam at the old tideline, lost
in our mouths: we will make even this a dangerous place.

NOT KNOTT'S NAOMI

No, not her, but neither you. Some nether Naomi,
newer, a weather, knuckled and narcotic, a pearly

nautilus at home in hard nacre. Not nude, no, but naked,
lying unclothed hidden by bedclothes. Underneath

you both moves another Naomi, nimble even now at night,
but revenant, lyric, a trick of the light. Veil over veil,

layered Naomis, wolves in the nettle, denying
the naming, howling how I'll know of them nothing.

MY MOTHER'S BOTTLE OF SCOTCH

Driving the bridge to work, I want to call and tell her
you and I are fighting—slow anger blunt as some beetle
nosing to nothing but one more inch in the world.

Over the rail, down that last fall that sometimes sings
my name, the pewter bay is the whorled skin at her throat,

and maybe I'd tell her instead how it shines there
near her breath. But when I turn, she's back at the counter
filling her glass from the nearly empty bottle in its usual place.

AS WE WATCH OUR EMPIRE'S END

These clouds rolling the dome of our world are our last
clouds. Not aware it's already after, we turn

to kiss each other—despite all these years of counting
wrongs—because our fragile tendons are so close

to the surface at the wrist and where the neck
meets the body. We let the grim slashes life has abraded

in our foreheads and around our mouths soften.
Relieved, finally, of all that we've wasted ourselves holding.

ALL THE WILD HIDES

—for LB2

This poem began as one of your poems, as so many have, with opium
and pin-pupiled animals, with gypsum, dresses, and horses.

I'm trying again what you taught me: To build a body to tend
with witches in wet dirt. To stir up a poison that'll kill over a lifetime.

But it's not working, and this is mine, too, so I demand:
You can't have died. But you did die and that, too late, reminded me

how I've missed you. I'm riding a rowboat through the ocean
without you but to you, looking anywhere but to where I pull.

TO PEEL SOD OR MUCK IN REED ROOTS
WITH CATFISH BELLIES

and find something wonderful to believe, and believe it's for me
if I just hold my hands out like this. To find it not in the sidewalk's

smell or in the riotous emptiness we've retrained through LCDs.
To find that one thing unbought: the snap of your heel

at the threshold; cold water's quench in the nighttime; your old
perfume bottle from drawer deep. To hold, to be held, pick wonder

as a crab from between the rocks with seaweed. Find it, claws and all—
a glimpse of pink, and see that I could let this rule me instead.

HEAVY

I heard the word *biopsy* today. And saw what was hidden,
like the bridge's footing. My own end inside,

a curled bat hinged to my rafters. There's a number
of times left I'll breath in this place. I want to apologize
for what I was: err and armor, knifed and knuckled.
But my alms melt as snow to the sun. I can't pay all

that I owe, so it'll just weigh in me the same way
the carbon in my body is the weight of my ashes.

NOW THAT THE TIME FOR LIVES
GETTING BETTER IS DONE

Sometimes I think there are no more happy stories in me, but
do you know there's a quasar named ULAS J1120+0641? It's nearly
29 billion light years away. That such a thing is, and we get to know.

And if I turned to you now, my one wet muscle run dry, would you
turn to me? And what else could my heart be for if not to try?
So far away, we only see the image of the quasar as it was

at the beginning. It's burned out now, the fact of its death already
riding toward us, hidden behind all the light that has ever been.

EVERY ENDING SHOULD MAKE
A SOUND

Fur should make a sound, pursing lips should. When a pupil
dilates or a chimney swift dives. The urn, full of what a person

was. Paint, old wool, the mountain. We should. Every reliquary,
every fault, every grave should make a sound. Vines of how

they hold up the ruin. All the people who were here with us
and now aren't. Dark should. This room. Dirt about

what it knows of what's now in the urn. Lines as they
break the edges of a mouth. Any last day spent alone.

TODAY I WANTED TO TRY HAPPINESS

When you read to me of another Celsius endpoint passed, I have trouble

rightly arranging my face. I should only show sadness, but after us also means

more landbound birds, more kids standing, fresh from the womb on four

graceless legs, to climb the cliff-face rather than into a pen. Such wonder

we'll leave behind, if we're quick enough to destroy us without destroying

all the rest first. I do want us to hold on until my children get to show

their children a wren, but I'm jealous of those last few who, at the start

of our unpreying after, will witness how easily the world lives without us.

PERSIMMONS

Lifting my daughter as she pinches the rusted needlenose pliers
    so the persimmon pops free.
The pliers cut my cheek as she hands it down. We aren't far
    from the spottily held fireline,
we don't know but it's jumped the road, moved on thicker
    growth that didn't burn
last year. There's no smell yet but the air's fuller, as on a bus
    with all its bodies
and the warm engine below. I let her slide down my back,
    remembering, as each time,
the time my father forgot the flathead screwdriver in his pocket
    that split my brother's chest.
I can't remember his scar, only the story. Was this the last time
    I'd lift her? It's too late
in the season for persimmons, they've already gone to dusk,
    the orchard lifts as it burns.

FOUR

ELEGY IN LIMESTONE

If the water, everywhere, and if she

is. If ghosts, like water, like if all

rivers and oceans and rains are one

ghost, surrounding and throughout.

If she is, like if the lakes and bays

of Seattle define Seattle, if the ices

of Mars and Massachusetts,

hidden in their deep stones, define

Mars and Massachusetts; if she is.

A thirst unmet, alkaline or saline,

the water not touching that thirst,

if my thirst wants something else

entirely. If she is. Water, if it is in

and is blood. If invisible until

exhale. If science lies and water

doesn't reflect sky but sky this

water. If she is the sound, if it isn't

essential until its lack. If she is

the sound of. Waves. If in the body,

the dew in morning, and the moon.

If she is the sound of the water.

If rising, if breaking, if throughout.

WITHIN THE CINDER THE SPARK

We're not yet at the end of gray
history. The fuses lit long ago

still flare through the streets.
The fast-moving faces behind

the shadows are still set to strike,
and more dogs will be untethered.

Perch in the high branches,
above where the ropes stripped

the bark, so you can be a witness
to whatever comes next.

I own a part of this.
Don't skirt the festering things,

the concertina wire and sidearms
that separate, the ashes

of set fires rising as black birds
from timothy fields.

When you wake in the shivering
dark, sit up and wait. Maybe

you'll be a witness when the air
thins of its noise. Maybe you'll be

a witness when the first blue
hacks open the night along its center.

COLONY COLLAPSE

From my moment I only see machines.
No walking in the yews, no knowing
the piano or Borges or clover.

Too fragile to view are those organic
architectures that grow in silk houses,
those myths from within the copses.

Works and reactors are uncountable,
unaccountable, and the dragonflies
of highways don't rest. Once,

I knew a story about Saturn
seen from there. A story about night
in Vermont. These stories, in buried

bones, won't be told again.
I don't know how we last so much
as a single day. Unless it's enough

I knew you. Didn't I? Naked in that
open field, unhidden. We were bigger
than all of mankind's metal gods.

INQUIRY INTO STORM

Just for today, let's erupt
the reverie with a plosive,

play in the halation,
the emblazoned, the significant

spiral of our specific
tornado. Today, let's

put on the facets of fallen
snowflakes, the skittered legs

of a young foal. Let's escape
into mottle, be a huge

and black blossom
amid all that unremarkable

greenery. Just for today,
shelving the hoax of polish

and supine, let's endure
as a mosquito's whir

and be the unexpected sweet
at the marrow of citrus.

INQUIRY INTO VESPER

The moon is curled within
its silver-fur blankets,

the dogs of day have circled
around their bodies, the door

is set to, the switch crashed
down. I'm a bright yellow-

and-black worker bee at rest
in his well-appointed cell.

I'm the weight of all the sand
as it nestles in the upturned

bell of the hourglass.
In the day's absence

is a caroming quiet,
which I attend to from

your collarbone's shallow
culvert. I am lucky.

And when the bats break
from the chimneys,

their sharp, echolocating
calls cut holes in the sky,

and I get to hear through
to the bright side.

INQUIRY INTO COTTON

In instinct, the animal
tide. In the mouth
of an open bloom

so heavy it's pulled
back below. In gristle,
sinew, the poisonously

rich muscle. In nerves,
bundled into ropes
to carry the touch

faster. In the dopamine
reward. In want
held within the lizard

mind, in swing,
and suck, and fear
of fire. In an androgynous

limb, unidentifiable
by bedlight. In losing
in licking, losing

in the private cry. In
coming inside into
our secret room of hands.

INQUIRY INTO APRICOT

I forgot that voice like licorice,
and legs, coltish. This hip,

right here, is not that hip,
I forgot that hip, sharp

as salted berries. The way
I forgot the blue until wind

rolled the fog, allowing.
That I knew, I knew it, just

there. But waters close
their mouths, and I might

never have seen anything
but gray. Your back, long

as an untested trestle bridge.
Your neck, long as a war year.

I forgot you. Until when you.
And you were blue, and it

wasn't too late, was not.
But too savage to ever stay.

GOODNIGHT TO THE TITANS

They drifted down
onto our town while we slept.
Their bayonets

shone in the white skirts
of our streetlights as they laced
our graveyards

with landmines and broke
the continuity of our streets
with cement

barricades. We wake
to a changed place, where we
need to be brave,

but our shoulders
are too slim to heft this new
and heavier world.

So we let the war settle
itself around us. We are home
with roving troops.

We watch their broken
young faces. And at night,
still too slim

to even light a candle
at the window, we whisper
goodnight

to the tank commanders
and infantrymen. Goodnight
to electrical outages,

bulldozers, and wires
spun with razors. Goodnight
tigers and weaving

spiders and goodnight
to all the occupiers. We hope
you find respite from

our shared brittleness,
from seeing what is your
only life as well.

STILL LIFE WITH LOVE AND NO LIGHTS

When alleycats. When chemicals run
stormdrains, when all the lovely balconies

are left empty. When powerlines wince
with the burden of occupying,

and in the blackberries dart coyotes.
When spiderwebs complicate. And also:

kissing. Yes. And why not a panther—
gloss in a body, gloss in arrogant

pantherhood. When trainyard
and truckstop beds, breakwater and red.

When it folds open, the rule-less rile
of sky, the comets and giants. And also:

books, chamomile, and more kissing.
In this, one less of only so many moons.

THE DANDELIONS IN THE MOMENT AND THEN

It is. And needles don't fall,
cones don't fall. The soil keeps

holding the grass seed and the dune
sand beneath is still torn by thirsty,

wooden hands. By bedrock
is where will be my tenoned pine.

And the grass seeds don't split,
their shoots don't spill. The clouds

remain, widely. That locked closet
inside will never have its tumblers

turned. Honestly, all I had
was the only lie—that I could be

the one who evades. Sparrows
don't fall, no owl falls. Left behind

are her thin hands, a box full
of ribbons, a bolt, a knife.

Photographs with anybody's faces.
Hungry letters, angry letters about

a time and people and love that is
not. No image holds its meaning

within itself. Not one dandelion fell.
Please. Something did happen here.

ACKNOWLEDGMENTS

Thanks to the editors of the following journals where some of these poems first appeared, some in different forms and some with different titles: *The Adroit Journal*, *Cimarron Review*, *Cincinnati Review*, *Colorado Review*, *Conjunctions* Online Exclusives, *Cortland Review*, *Crazyhorse*, *Denver Quarterly*, *Gulf Coast*, *Handsome*, *Hayden's Ferry Review*, *Little Star*, *Massachusetts Review*, *Poetry Northwest*, *Sixth Finch*, and *Tin House*. Thanks also to the Academy of American Poets for including "Elegy in Limestone" and "The dandelions in the moment and then" in their Poem-a-Day program, *Poetry Daily* for republishing "Jupiter Is Blind," and *Little Star Weekly* and the Poetry Society of America for republishing "Within the Cinder the Spark," This book was written with support from the miracle that is the Amy Lowell Poetry Traveling Scholarship.

There are too many influences on these poems to list, and I'm sure there are many echoes of which I'm not even aware, so I'd like to thank the poets. All of you. Directly (or nearly directly) quoted here are works by Lorine Niedecker, William Shakespeare, and John Keats. "Trying To Hear a Hymn to Life" is after poems called "Hymn to Life" by Timothy Donnelly and James Schuyler, and also nods to poems of the same title by Lou Andreas-Salomé and Nazim Hikmet.

Thanks to Crystal Williams, Maxine Scates, and Lisa Steinman for guidance and encouragement at the pivot point. To Terrance Hayes for essential early support, to Don Mee Choi, Phillip B. Williams, and Ilya Kaminsky for lending their words and valuable time. And to Lucie Brock-Broido, who gave so much to me and so many others.

I'd like to thank Victoria Chang for her beautiful introduction, for her work in the poetry community at large, and most of all for her poems, which have meant a great deal to me for many years. And to the staff of Sarabande, who take such care and make gorgeous books.

Finally, thanks to my family and friends, near and far, lost and present.

CJ EVANS is the author of *A Penance* (New Issues Press) and *The Category of Outcast*, selected by Terrance Hayes for the Poetry Society of America's Chapbook Fellowship. A past recipient of the Amy Lowell Poetry Traveling Scholarship, he currently lives in California, where he is the editorial director of Two Lines Press, a publisher of international literature in translation.